England without a King
1649–1660

IN THE SAME SERIES

General Editors: Eric J. Evans and P.D. King

LANCASTER PAMPHLETS

England without a King 1649–1660

Austin Woolrych

London and New York

First published 1983 by
Methuen & Co. Ltd

Reprinted 1993, 1995
by Routledge
11 New Fetter Lane, London EC4P 4EE
29 West 35th Street, New York, NY 10001

Typeset in Great Britain by
Scarborough Typesetting Services
Printed in Great Britain by
Clays Ltd, St Ives plc

British Library Cataloguing in Publication Data
Woolrych, Austin
England without a king 1649–1660. – (Lancaster pamphlets; 1)
1. Great Britain – History – Puritan Revolution,
1642–1660
I. Title   II. Series
942.06'3   DA405
ISBN 0–415–10456–4

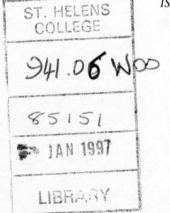

Contents

Foreword

Lancaster Pamphlets offer concise and up-to-date accounts of major historical topics, primarily for the help of students preparing for Advanced Level examinations, though they should also be of value to those pursuing introductory courses in universities and other institutions of higher education. They do not rely on prior textbook knowledge. Without being all-embracing, their aims are to bring some of the central themes or problems confronting students and teachers into sharper focus than the textbook writer can hope to do; to provide the reader with some of the results of recent research which the textbook may not embody; and to stimulate thought about the whole interpretation of the topic under discussion. They are written by experienced university scholars who have a strong interest in teaching.

At the end of this pamphlet is a numbered list of the recent or fairly recent works that the writer considers most relevant to his subject. Where a statement or a paragraph is particularly indebted to one or more of these works, the number is given in the text in brackets. This serves at the same time to acknowledge the writer's source and to show the reader where he may find a more detailed exposition of the point concerned.

Time chart

1646 May: Charles I gives himself up to the Scots at Newcastle.

June: first Civil War ends with surrender of Oxford.

July: parliament sends peace propositions to the king at Newcastle.

1647 January: Scottish army withdraws from England and hands over Charles I.

April–
May: regiments of the New Model Army elect Agitators.

June: New Model Army defies parliament's orders for its disbandment and captures Charles I.

July: army formulates *Heads of the Proposals* and submits them to Charles.

Late Oct.–
early Nov.:   'Putney Debates' between officers, Agitators and Levellers over the first *Agreement of the People*.

11 Nov.:   Charles escapes from the army and makes for Isle of Wight.

15 Nov.:   abortive Leveller mutiny of two regiments at Corkbush Field.

26 Dec.:   Charles signs Engagement with Scottish commissioners.

1648	January:	parliament breaks off negotiations (Vote of No Addresses).
	April:	insurgents in south Wales declare for the king.
	May–June:	Fairfax defeats Kentish insurgents and besieges those of Essex in Colchester.
	July:	Cromwell stamps out south Wales rising; Scottish army enters England.
	17 Aug.:	Cromwell destroys Scottish army at Preston; 27 Aug., Colchester surrenders.
	18 Sep.:	Treaty of Newport opens.
	6 Dec.:	Pride's Purge.
1649	30 Jan.:	execution of Charles I.
	March:	Acts abolishing monarchy and House of Lords.
	14 May:	defeat of Leveller mutineers at Burford.
	19 May:	Act declaring England to be a Commonwealth.
	July:	Cromwell departs for Ireland.
1650	2 Jan.:	Engagement to be faithful to the Commonwealth imposed on all male adults.
	June:	Cromwell returns from Ireland; Charles II sails for Scotland; Fairfax resigns, and Cromwell succeeds him as Lord General.
	July:	Cromwell leads army into Scotland.
	3 Sep.:	Battle of Dunbar.
	27 Sep.:	Act to repeal the penal laws compelling attendance at parish churches.
1651	3 Sep.:	Battle of Worcester.
	9 Oct.:	Rump passes Navigation Act.

1652	June:	outbreak of first Anglo-Dutch war.
	13 Aug.:	Council of Officers presents strong petition to Rump.
	14 Sep.:	Rump appoints committee to submit a 'bill for a new representative'.
1653	23 Feb.:	'bill for a new representative' placed before Rump by Haselrig.
	20 April:	Cromwell expels the Rump.
	4 July:	opening of 'Barebone's Parliament'.
	12 Dec.:	resignation of Barebone's Parliament.
	16 Dec.:	installation of Cromwell as Lord Protector.
1654	April:	peace signed with Dutch Republic.
	3 Sep.:	first parliament of the Protectorate assembles.
1655	22 Jan.:	Cromwell dissolves parliament.
	March:	Penruddock's Rising.
	May:	conquest of Jamaica.
	Aug.–Oct.:	regime of major-generals established throughout England (until Jan. 1657).
	October:	Spain declares war.
1656	17 Sep.:	second parliament of the Protectorate assembles.
1657	23 Feb.:	proposal in parliament to make Cromwell king under a new constitution.
	31 March:	Humble Petition and Advice presented to Cromwell.
	8 May:	Cromwell finally refuses the crown.
	26 June:	Cromwell reinstalled as Protector under Humble Petition and Advice.
1658	20 Jan.–4 Feb.:	second session and dissolution of second Protectorate parliament.

	14 June:	Battle of the Dunes, followed by acquisition of Dunkirk.
	3 Sep.:	death of Oliver Cromwell; Richard Cromwell proclaimed Protector.
1659	27 Jan.:	third Protectorate parliament assembles.
	22 April:	army commanders force Richard to dissolve parliament.
	7 May:	Rump recalled; end of Protectorate.
	13 Oct.:	army again interrupts the Rump; Committee of Safety (27 Oct.).
	26 Dec.:	Rump again returns to power.
1660	1 Jan.:	Monck begins his march to London.
	21 Feb.:	Monck readmits the Secluded Members.
	16 March:	Long Parliament dissolves itself.
	25 April:	Convention Parliament assembles.
	8 May:	Charles II proclaimed king.

England without a King 1649–1660

Stages on the road to a scaffold

The story of the English Commonwealth properly begins with the execution of a king and the establishment of a republic. But why did England ever become a republic at all? That is the first problem, for no one imagined such an outcome when the Civil War began. The Long Parliament went to war in 1642 'for king and parliament', and even five years later, when Charles I was parrying all the conditions that it sought to impose on him after his defeat, very few members of either House contemplated abolishing the monarchy. When the New Model Army defied the orders for its disbandment and carried him off, in that same year, 1647, it proceeded to offer him fairer terms for his restoration than the parliament had done. The anti-monarchical movement in the army had as yet barely begun.

Nor does the explanation lie in any rapid conversion of parliamentary politicians to revolutionary doctrines. It used to be thought that after the army purged the Long Parliament in December 1648, the Rump that was left was a pretty radical body; but Professor Underdown has shown that few of these Rumpers were republicans by conviction at the time when they set up the republic (29), and Dr Worden has further demonstrated how few genuine revolutionaries there were even in the original core of members who put the king on trial for his life (42). There was a sprinkling of true radicals in London and the provinces who petitioned for justice on the king, but most of the country was

1

appalled by his execution. The army bore a large responsibility for it, but the politics of the army had changed dramatically in the course of less than two years. Dr Kishlansky has argued that the New Model was not a radical body in origin, but first became politicized during 1647 (15–17), and it was not until late in 1648 that its officers agreed in pressing for capital charges against the king (29). Among the minority of Englishmen who concurred with them, many did so not because they rejected monarchy as such, but because they felt that Charles himself had left them nowhere else to go.

Historians are shy of attributing vast consequences to one person's decisions, but Charles really gives them no choice. He took a huge gamble at the end of 1647, and he lost. Since July the army commanders had been offering him, in the Heads of the Proposals, terms as honourable as he could reasonably expect, and his shrewdest advisers urged him to close with them. Instead, he went on trying to play the army off against the parliament, and then proceeded to jilt both in favour of new proposals that some high-ranking commissioners brought him from Scotland. There, power had been shifting from the strict Covenanters led by the Marquis of Argyll, who would not help him unless he personally swore to the Solemn League and Covenant and confirmed the newly established Presbyterian Church of England, to the rival aristocratic faction headed by his old councillor the Duke of Hamilton. Hamilton's party, being concerned more about preserving the nobility's ascendancy than about Presbyterianism, was prepared to give Charles military aid without making him take the Covenant or bow to irksome political restraints. Regarding religion, they only asked him to confirm Presbyterianism in England for three years. Charles was powerfully drawn; he escaped from the army's custody to the Isle of Wight in November so that he could negotiate with the Scotsmen without the English generals breathing down his neck. That was too much for the army leaders, who had lately been in conflict with some radical 'agitators' who opposed any further traffic with him. The army closed its ranks. Charles proceeded to sign a secret Engagement with the Scots on 26 December, whereby they would send him an army and he would call the English royalists to arms again. The result was to be the second Civil War.

2

But could Hamilton deliver the army that he promised, and would the cavaliers rise again? Hamilton got his answer when the best Scottish officers declined to serve and the Presbyterian ministers cursed his poor conscript rabble from their pulpits because it was going to fight for an uncovenanted king. He was forced to assume the command himself. He was encouraged in the spring of 1648 by news of risings in Kent and Essex and South Wales, but they were inspired not so much by any positive enthusiasm for the king as by hatred of the local agencies of the Long Parliament's rule, especially its now notorious county committees (9, 22). The royalists tried to harness these local uprisings to the king's cause, but it all happened too early for them to join forces with Hamilton's invasion, which was delayed by the difficulties he had in raising and training a Scottish army at all. Cromwell had time to stamp out the insurgents in South Wales, and Fairfax to corner those from Kent and Essex in Colchester, before the Scots even crossed the border. Cromwell fell on Hamilton's army at Preston on 17 August with a force half its size, and in a three-day running fight he annihilated it (36). Colchester then surrendered, Cromwell's army restored Argyll to power in Scotland and the second Civil War was over.

But victory in arms did not resolve the situation in England. Despite the duplicity that Charles had shown towards everyone who treated with him, and despite his having plunged two kingdoms into a fruitless new war, the majority of his subjects – the majority even of those who had initially sided against him – would rather have seen him back on his throne, even without all the safeguards they required, than leave the country's future in the hands of the army and its political allies. It was not only because they clung to the ancient constitution and nursed exaggerated fears that the country would be sacrificed to Levelling democracy in the state, and sectarian anarchy in the church, if the army and its supporters had their way. England was also impoverished and war-weary. Not only had the wars brought heavy casualties, widespread destruction and an unprecedented weight of taxation, but armies on both sides had often been driven to help themselves to food, quarters, horses and money. Many gentlemen who had first sided with parliament because it stood for law and

3

property had become alienated when the harsh demands of war rode roughshod over both. Large and expensive forces were still afoot, and though they had all at last been brought under Fairfax's command in July 1647 they were by no means all as well disciplined as the New Model Army (23). Many regions had had the experience of unpaid troops living at free quarter. With violent clashes between soldiers and local countrymen, growing numbers of disbanded men roaming without employment and riotous attacks on the detested collectors of the excise, 1647 and 1648 were years in which law and order were precarious and the threat of social revolution loomed darkly. To make matters worse, the harvests in both years were disastrous and food at times approached famine prices. The sufferings of the poorer classes tended to make them yearn nostalgically for the old ways, while the well-to-do gentry chafed because their traditional authority as justices of the peace and in other local commissions had been largely usurped by upstart committee-men who took their orders from Westminster. The latter were often, though not always, of lower social rank, but what made the county committees most unpopular was that they put the central government's interest above that of the county and kept on imposing the heavy financial burdens of the war years (9, 22, 29).

The second Civil War had two main effects: it deepened the political divisions in parliament and it made the army's politics much more radical. At Westminster, the interval between the two wars had been dominated by strife between political factions known as Presbyterians and Independents, though they did not correspond at all closely to the religious denominations which went by the same names. During 1647 the main issue between them had been that the Presbyterians wanted to reinstate the king and get the New Model Army disbanded without delay, even if Charles offered less than satisfactory constitutional concessions and only a temporary acceptance of the Presbyterian religious settlement, whereas the Independents aimed to keep the army afoot until he had been firmly bound to conditions which would secure the ends for which they had fought, including (for the army at least) liberty of conscience (15, 29). So far only a handful of ultra-radical MPs had any thought of a settlement without the king, but their number was increased by his deliberate renewal of civil war.

Even so, the majority clung to the hope and intention of retaining Charles as king, under strict constitutional restraints. To most people, inside and outside parliament, the second Civil War presented a miserable choice of evils. They wanted to preserve the monarchy, but to have had Charles borne back to power by the swords of a Scottish army would have meant that the restraints on him would be minimal. It could have launched a counter-revolution that would have swept away the precious reforms that the king had conceded in 1641, and led to political death for all who had acted in the parliamentary cause. Yet an out-and-out triumph for the army threatened the abolition of monarchy itself, and of many other ancient institutions. Understandably, the parliament's course seemed to waver. In January 1648, when Charles had virtually rejected the parliament's propositions, but before his Engagement with the Scots was publicly known, both Houses passed the Vote of No Addresses, thereby formally breaking off negotiations with him. Yet on 28 April, with a rising afoot in South Wales and with the Scots unmistakably preparing for war, the Commons declared that they would not alter 'the fundamental government of the kingdom by King, Lords and Commons'. The army reacted differently, only a day or two later. Officers and representatives of the soldiery met together for an emotional day of prayer before they took the field against the enemy in Wales, and they resolved 'that it was our duty, if ever the Lord brought us back again in peace, to call Charles Stuart, that man of blood, to an account for the blood he had shed . . . against the Lord's cause and people in these poor nations'.

A year earlier such a resolution by the Council of War would have been unthinkable. When the regiments first elected agitators to represent the soldiery's grievances they were generally well disposed towards the king; their quarrel was with the Presbyterian politians in parliament who sought to disband them with little regard for their rights or needs and seemed bent on a sell-out peace. Feeling hardened against the king in the autumn of 1647, partly because he played fast and loose with the army's proposals for restoring him, and partly because the Levellers were busy indoctrinating the soldiery with the ideal of a democratic republic, based on an Agreement of the People embodying the equal rights of all free-born citizens. Yet the commanders – Sir Thomas Fairfax the Lord General, Cromwell the Lieutenant-General, and Cromwell's son-in-law Commissary-General Ireton, the chief brain of what we would call the high command – were well in control of the army, which was still less permeated with radical politics than was generally feared. When the Levellers tried to raise a mutiny in support of the Agreement in November, only two regiments responded, and they were easily brought back to obedience. Many regiments who attended the rendezvous where this demonstration was attempted cried repeatedly 'For the king and Sir Thomas!'

But that was before Charles finally chose to resort to war rather than negotiation, and that choice naturally turned most of the army against him. It was the members of the army whose lives (amongst others) he gambled with, and many fell; furthermore, many officers and men believed that God had already pronounced against his cause. Despite that prayer meeting in April, by no means all felt committed yet to trying the king for his life, let alone abolishing the monarchy; Fairfax certainly did not, and neither, probably, did Cromwell (29). But all of them felt a growing indignation over the steps which the parliament took to seek a reconciliation with him, long before the outcome of the war was decided on the battlefield. Parliament acted so partly because of pressure from the City of London, where the Presbyterian clergy drummed up massive popular support for bringing the king back to his capital, and partly because fears of the army's intentions restored the ascendancy of the political Presbyterians at Westminster. The Houses voted on 24 May to resume treating with Charles if he accepted certain demands in advance. During June and July the main questions that occupied them were whether the negotiation should be at Westminster or on the Isle of Wight, and whether he should first have to grant the preliminary concessions that he had refused the previous December. In the event Charles did not, and less than a month after the Scottish army was wiped out at Preston a group of parliamentary commissioners met him on the Isle of Wight to commence the Treaty of Newport.

Not surprisingly, the army felt that the causes for which it had again risked life and limb were being bartered away, especially the cause of liberty of conscience, which was increasingly important to the army, but which was opposed by the Presbyterian politicians, the king and the Scots. At Newport Charles made concessions which, as he admitted to his confidants, he did not intend to honour. At Westminister the old Independent party was split, according to whether its members regarded a royalist reaction or the destruction of the ancient constitution as the greater danger, but MPs who openly opposed the treaty went in fear of their lives. The army was slow to intervene. Fairfax and some other relatively conservative officers shrank from offering violence to either an anointed king or an elected parliament. Cromwell, racked by conflicting feelings, avoided committing himself by lingering all through November over the siege of Pontefract, where an isolated royalist garrison held out forlornly. Ireton, however, knew his own mind, and he had most of the army behind him. He saw Charles as not only guilty of the recent war, but incorrigible, and he believed that unless the army intervened to stop the treaty, the civil and religious liberties that it had fought for would be signed away.

Ireton's first attempt to persuade the General Council of the Army (consisting now only of officers) to present an ultimatum to parliament was on 10 November, and it failed. Only on the 16th, probably after one more fruitless approach to Charles in order to satisfy his more conservative fellow-officers, did he get the General Council to approve a crucial Remonstrance, calling on parliament to break off negotiation and bring the king to trial. Ireton was now being troubled on his other flank by the Levellers, who had revived and strengthened their influence on the soldiery in recent months. They demanded that the army should not move against either the king or the parliament until it had committed itself to establishing a democratic commonwealth, based on an Agreement of the People which every well-affected citizen should be invited to sign. Reluctantly, to avoid dissension in the army's ranks at this critical stage, he agreed that a committee of Levellers, officers, MPs and London Independents – four of each group – should draft a new version of the Agreement, less extreme

7

(he hoped) and more specific than the one that had caused such conflict a year ago.

Ireton's plan at the end of November, as the army prepared for action, was that it should dissolve the parliament and recognize the members who opposed the Newport Treaty as a provisional government for as long as it would take to arrange general elections and assemble a new parliament. But these members would not give their consent to a dissolution by military force, even though they wanted the treaty stopped. They insisted that the army should merely shut out the MPs who were pursuing a pact with the king and should recognize the rest as still constituting a valid parliament. Ireton had to submit, and the result was Pride's Purge. On 5 December both Houses voted that the king's answers to their proposed terms were 'a ground to proceed upon' for settling the kingdom. The next day MPs found the parliament-house beset by troops under Colonel Pride, who arrested many leading Presbyterians and prevented many others from entering. Ireton only told Fairfax, his general, about this *coup* when he had set it all up and it was about to begin. Cromwell arrived in London from Pontefract, 'a reluctant accomplice', on the evening of the 6th when the purge was an accomplished fact. Only a small minority of members were at first prepared to go on acting after this act of military violence, and still not all of them were convinced that the king should be put on trial. Cromwell himself was not; he and other moderate Independents tried until Christmas to find a compromise whereby most of the purged members could return to their seats, and he went on seeking some alternative to the act of regicide until well into the new year (29).

But neither Charles nor the hard core of revolutionaries in both army and parliament were interested in compromise by now, and when Cromwell realized it he became as implacable as anyone. What was left of the House of Commons – the Rump, as it came to be called – voted for a High Court of Justice to try the king for waging war on his people, which it construed as high treason. The handful of peers who still attended the House of Lords refused to concur; whereupon the Rump resolved 'that the people are, under God, the original of all just power, [and] that the Commons of England . . . being chosen by and representing the people, have the supreme power in this nation'. Such was the basis of the Commonwealth, a basis from which no solid structure was to grow.

England's new masters

It has needed a narrative to explain how England, against the wishes of most of the political nation, came to be a republic. From this point, however, there can be no attempt to tell a continuous story of the Commonwealth's affairs. Readers who want to come to grips with the latest work on its detailed political history, its foreign relations and its dealings with Ireland and Scotland are referred to the following works in the bibliography: 2, 4, 8, 14, 27, 34, 42. In what follows the emphasis will be on the general character of the successive regimes between Pride's Purge and the Restoration, and on the tensions and weaknesses that made each of them short-lived.

We begin with the Rump, which wielded supreme authority until Cromwell expelled it in 1653. Thanks to Underdown and Worden, we now know how very diverse its membership was. Only about seventy members identified themselves actively with its exercise of power in the crucial weeks between Pride's Purge and the king's execution on 30 January 1649, and only forty-three signed his death warrant. The rest of the regicides were non-members; their total number was seventy, for, besides the fifty-nine who signed, there were eleven more who assented to the death sentence at the last session of the High Court of Justice (20). The original Rumpers included genuine revolutionaries like Marten and Ludlow, but some of them were more conservative figures who sat on largely to maintain a parliamentary presence and prevent a take-over of power by the army.

The Rump would have remained tiny if only those who publicly approved the king's execution had been allowed to sit, but from 1 February it admitted any member who would register his dissent from the Commons' vote on 5 December that the king's response to the Newport terms provided grounds for a peace settlement. That decision brought back at least thirty members in a day, and over eighty by early March; they included the Speaker, William Lenthall, and two of the Rump's leading politicians, Sir Arthur Haselrig and Sir Henry Vane the younger. There were some genuine radicals among these 'February dissenters' who had held aloof from the proceedings against the king, but most were of a more conservative stamp than the Rump's original core. The chief concern of many of them was that power should not fall into the hands of soldiers, Levellers, sectaries or any other kind of revolutionary. That was truer still of the fifty or so who returned to their seats later than February (29, 42).

Well over two hundred members sat in the Rump at one time or another, including ten whom by-elections brought in, but only about a third attended at all regularly. The average number prsent, judging by the votes in divisions, remained between fifty and sixty throughout its existence (42).

It used to be said that Pride's Purge removed the political Presbyterians (which it did) and left the Independents in power. But Underdown has demonstrated that the Independents lost all coherence as a political group during 1648, and the label has little meaning thereafter except in its original religious sense. In that sense there were at least as many Presbyterians as Independents and sectaries in the Rump. The inauguration of the Commonwealth coincided with a great outburst of radical religious enthusiasm; 1649 was a formative year for the Fifth Monarchy men and the Quakers, as it was for the Diggers and the Ranters (6, 12). But most of the Rumpers were as appalled by these manifestations as their fellow-gentry in their counties were. The army had been hoping for a new, more tolerant and evangelical settlement of religion, but in August the Rump debated a proposal to confirm the exclusive, intolerant Presbyterian Church of England that the parliament had tried to establish from 1645 onwards. The Yeas and Noes were exactly equal, and only the Speaker's casting vote rejected it. Not until September 1650, and then only under army pressure, did the Rump repeal the Elizabethan statutes compelling attendance at Sunday worship in the established church, and the toleration thus grudgingly granted was restricted by a Blasphemy Act passed in the previous month. The Rump was no more radical in religion than in politics, and its attitude to the sects grew colder as time went on.

Its reluctance to innovate already appeared within days of the king's death, when it debated whether to abolish the House of Lords. Only a handful of peers still attended, and a hereditary upper house had no logical place in a state which had declared the people's representatives to be sovereign. Yet some members, Cromwell among them, wanted it to remain with an advisory role in the legislative process, and they were beaten only by forty-four votes to twenty-nine. Only after that did the Rump debate 'whether kingship should be abolished or not', and only in May 1649 did it formally enact that England should 'be governed as a Commonwealth and free state . . . without any king or House of Lords'. The word 'republic' was studiously avoided, and never can a republic have been established with so few really convinced republicans among its founding fathers.

The Rump showed its prevailing conservatism just as clearly when it chose its first Council of State in mid-February. Thirty-four of the forty-one councillors were MPs, and they included only twelve regicides. Of the other seven, five were peers. Ireton and Thomas Harrison, the officers most responsible for Pride's Purge and the next most influential men in the army after Fairfax and Cromwell, were nominated for appointment, but rejected by the House. The council was appointed for a year only and subjected to Parliament's jealous control. Three intentions were plain already: to cover up the regime's revolutionary origins, to delegate as little power as possible, and to keep the army out of politics.

The army had grown into a genuinely radical body, though by no means uniformly so. Perhaps its least radical member was its general. Fairfax was unhappy and undecided all through the train of events that brought the Commonwealth into being, but he did not bring himself to resign until June 1650. Only then did Cromwell become commander-in-chief, and it was and is a common error to credit him with more political power than he actually wielded and with more radical views than he really held. As a member of parliament and of the council he commanded great respect, but neither body was subject to his will, and both could and did take decisions that he deplored. There was also a certain conflict within him between the religious enthusiasm that he shared with his old comrades in the New Model cavalry and the largely traditional political and social attitudes that he shared with his fellow gentry. He had faced the prospect of executing the king reluctantly, until he became convinced that providence itself had pronounced sentence. His son-in-law Ireton, who had the keenest political brain and the strongest political initiative in the army, had grasped the grim logic of that deed much earlier. But though Ireton might look like a revolutionary to the outraged majority of political Englishmen, he was in fact a constitutionalist. He believed that the nation's accumulated political wisdom was distilled in fundamental laws of great antiquity, including one which confined the right to vote to men of some small property. He had pursued the king to death not because he was opposed to monarchy in principle, but because of what Charles I had done. That distinguished him from the many officers who were by now doctrinaire republicans, and still more from the Levellers in the army, who wanted to wipe the constitutional slate clean and start afresh on the basis of an Agreement of the People. There was also another quite different strain of radicalism in the army, inspired by millenarianism. The most extreme millenarians were the Fifth Monarchy men, of whom more will be said shortly. They grew in strength from 1649 onwards, thanks largely to the championship of that flamboyant, God-intoxicated man Major-General Harrison.

The defeat of radical hopes

At the time of Pride's Purge the Levellers inside and outside the army rested their hopes on the new Agreement of the People which had just been framed by the mixed committee described earlier. They expected that the army commanders would put it first to the regiments and then to the whole body of the people, who by signing *en masse* would make it the binding and unalterable constitution of the Commonwealth. To their disgust, the General Council of the Army (consisting only of officers) debated it on and off for a month in the so-called Whitehall Debates and introduced considerable changes in it. The Leveller leaders were exasperated; they saw this as a smokescreen to cover the setting up of a new tyranny, and they pulled out in indignation. To be fair, most of the amendments that the officers made were aimed not at wrecking the Agreement but at making it more workable and acceptable. The main difference arose because Ireton insisted, as Cromwell would have done, that there should be an established church and ministry maintained by the Commonwealth, though Protestants who dissented from it should be free to worship their own way.

But while most of the officers on the General Council probably took the Agreement seriously as a blueprint for the Commonwealth's future government, the senior commanders almost certainly disliked it. They were totally unwilling to go over the heads of the parliament and appeal to the people directly, though whether the majority of the people would have welcomed the Agreement and signed it is a very open question. They presented it to the Rump on 20 January in the form of a petition, and they imposed no further pressure to get it implemented. They probably counted on it being laid quietly to sleep, and that is what happened. One may well feel regret that this considered programme for a substantial degree of democracy was shuffled aside so soon, for alongside some impracticalities it had many merits; but to wish that it could have broadened the Commonwealth's foundations and built bridges between moderates and radicals is to wish that the leaders in both the army and the parliament had been other men than they were.

The Levellers erupted in bitter protest against what they saw as a cheat. In their eyes, the army grandees had installed an oligarchy of hostile, anti-democratic politicians in supreme power as partners in a military tyranny. Angry pamphlets called upon the people, and especially the soldiery, to resist, and soon their leaders were imprisoned in the Tower. From there they complained in *A Manifestation* that the Commonwealth's masters were squandering the best opportunity in six hundred years – i.e. since before the Norman Conquest – 'of making this a truly happy and wholly free nation', and contriving that 'the change be only notional, nominal, circumstantial, whilst the real burdens, grievances, and bondages, be continued, even when the monarchy is changed into a republic' (1). Those Levellers still at liberty put all their efforts into raising a major mutiny in the army, and on May Day they published a new, uncompromising Agreement of the People as its manifesto.

The May mutiny was more serious than that in November 1647, but the Levellers never won over anything like enough soldiers to stand a chance of success. Their strength in a few regiments was enough to bring out Fairfax and Cromwell to lead the loyal units against them, but on 14 May the last four hundred mutineers surrendered after a pathetic little skirmish at Burford. With notable lenience only one ringleader was shot, though Fairfax and Cromwell had probably noted how skilfully the Levellers capitalized on their martyrs. Thereafter the whole movement rapidly lost its momentum and coherence, though Lilburne went on campaigning in print until he was exiled, and even then he staged a brief come-back in 1653.

It is worth pausing to ask why this, the most serious call to popular revolution before the Chartist movement, had so short a life. Its failure marked the critical point at which it was determined that the political revolution which had cut off the king's head was not to develop into a social revolution, of a kind that would radically alter the whole social basis of power in the state, or even dissolve (as Cromwell put it) 'the ranks and orders of men whereby England hath been known for hundreds of years'. It is not enough to say that the Levellers' objectives were centuries ahead of their time; the same would doubtless have been said of Lenin and Mao if they had failed. But therein lies a crucial difference. Lenin and Mao were not merely inspired by ideologies; they were genuine revolutionaries, with viable strategies for seizing and holding power and a ruthless resolve to pursue it. The Levellers had no such strategy, and strong reservations about resorting to force at all.

They had no hope of converting the established authorities by persuasion. Their many petitions to parliament served, when printed, to disseminate their ideas, but they only angered and alarmed the typical members of the Commons because they so plainly threatened their interests. Their famous demand for manhood suffrage in parliamentary elections was not so revolutionary as used to be thought, because the Commons themselves had been moving for many years towards upholding the right of every adult male inhabitant to vote in borough constituencies, which filled over four-fifths of the seats (13). In any case, the Levellers were prepared to compromise on manhood suffrage (3d), but when they demanded that all justices and other public officers in the counties and the towns should be elected by the people for one year and no longer, they sought to demolish at a stroke the traditional right of the major landed families to govern the counties and the wealthiest merchants to govern the towns. The Levellers strenuously renounced any intention to abolish property or level men's estates, but it is difficult to see how they could have achieved the political equality that they sought without changing the huge inequality of wealth and status that still existed in mid-seventeenth-century England.

The Levellers were in fact a precociously well-organized pressure group rather than a revolutionary movement, and much more interested in principles than in power. To the question who would have actually *governed* their republic between their biennial parliaments, i.e. for at least three-quarters of the time according to their own proposals, they seem to have given no thought until they sat down with more experienced politicians to draft the second Agreement. When their petitions and demonstrations made only a negative impact on the actual wielders of power, they had no strategy but to win over the army, and when they failed in that they rapidly faded.

It still has to be explained why most of the army resisted their call and why the strong popular support that they commanded for about two years, at any rate in London, did not keep them going longer. One reason is that when the 'middling sort' and lesser folk found their voice in the English Revolution it was not always a radical voice, as was shown by some of the Clubmen movements towards the end of the Civil War and by the crowds of London citizens who demonstrated for the recall of the king in 1647–8. Leveller radicalism may have alienated as many as it attracted. Moreover popular radicalism did not necessarily tend towards democracy; it could be caught up in the powerful current of millenarianism, which carried it in an almost opposite direction.

Very many puritans of all shades of opinion had for years been passionately engrossed in the scriptural prophecies, especially in Daniel and Revelation, concerning the future and final phases of the world's history. Foxe's Book of Martyrs had long taught Englishmen to identify the papacy with Antichrist, or the Beast, and to think of England as an elect nation, destined to play a heroic role in the final overthrow of Antichrist. More recently the downfall of Laud's and Charles I's 'tyranny', coupled with defeats of the Spanish and Imperial forces in the Thirty Years War, made many hope that that overthrow had already begun. 'God is decreeing to begin some new and great period in His Church,' wrote Milton in 1644; 'What does He then but reveal Himself to His servants, and as his manner is, first to his Englishmen?' The most extreme millenarians were the Fifth Monarchy men, whose rise began in 1649. Like others, they identified the four beasts in Daniel's dream with the four great empires of the ancient world, the fourth being the Roman, which the papacy had usurped; but to them Antichrist was personified not only in the papacy but in all worldly monarchies, especially that of Charles I. His execution was the signal for setting up the Fifth Monarchy, the reign of King Jesus. Christ, however, was to rule not in person, but through his saints, whose reign of a thousand years was foretold by Daniel. Only at the end of that millennium would Christ himself appear in majesty to judge the world and bring it to an end.

The Fifth Monarchists were not alone in believing that Christ's kingdom was imminent. What marked them off from saner millenarians was their conviction that it was to be a physical and highly authoritarian kingdom, and that the saints had a divine call to establish it by overturning all 'carnal' institutions, parliaments as well as kings, if necessary by force. The saints, of course, were themselves. They had no time for Leveller democracy, according to which all just power derived from the people. Parliaments could claim no such power, they declared, for the people had none to bestow; power derived only from Christ. 'How can the kingdom be the Saints',' asked one of their tracts in February 1649, 'when the ungodly are electors, and elected to govern?' But the Fifth Monarchists were not alone in turning against the Levellers, for other more sober Independent and Baptist congregations found their objectives too wordly and distrusted their egalitarianism. Some attacked them, quite unjustifiably, as atheists and libertines (6, 28).

Levellers and Fifth Monarchists were not the only types of radical to emerge in this time of ferment, when the old pillars of authority in church and state were collapsing and social barriers had been eroded by the brute facts of civil war. It was in the spring of 1649 that a group who called themselves True Levellers, but are better known as the Diggers, formed the first of several communes and tried to support themselves by collectively cultivating some common land in Surrey. Their leader Gerrard Winstanley had a vision of a secular millennium, to be achieved by making the earth once more 'a common treasury' for all. Man's original sin, he taught, had lain in carving out private property and imposing bondage on his fellow men, but the old Adam would be cast out and the promises of redemption would be fulfilled when men and women renounced all lordship, property and money, and lived by their common labours off the fruits of the earth. In the spirit of love they would be reborn; it was a demythologized version of the kingdom of Christ. But inevitably the Digger communes drew down the wrath of all property-owners, and within a year or two all that was left of their experiment were Winstanley's marvellous writings (35).

Winstanley's first few tracts were very close in spirit to the earliest Quakers (19), but from 1649 the two movements went their separate ways. The Quakers clashed with authority from the start, partly because they often interrupted church services and refused the conventional respects accorded to social superiors (especially magistrates), and partly because in Calvinist eyes their teaching that the 'inner light' of the spirit could have an authority above that of scripture was gravely heretical. But they did not carry their belief in inward illumination as far as the Ranters, who held that sin ceased to exist for men and women who attuned themselves fully to the godhead that they sensed within themselves. The Ranters' rejection of not only rank and property but of all conventional morality also brought down fierce persecution upon them, and unlike the Quakers they did not survive long beneath it.

17

These and other movements which germinated in the ferment that followed the Civil Wars have been lovingly and movingly described by Christopher Hill (12). Some of them made enduring contributions to the thought and experience of mankind, but it must be said that their impact on the actual course of the Commonwealth's history was slight. Some left-wing historians have written as though a great surge of potential revolutionary change was turned back when the Leveller mutinies were suppressed and the Digger communes broken up, or when Barebone's Parliament gave way to the Protectorate. But no really viable radical alternative was ever offered to a government based more or less on the traditional political nation of gentry and other property owners. Levellers, Diggers and Fifth Monarchy men pulled against each other; none had a plausible strategy for securing power or a sufficient social basis of support from which to exercise it. Quakers and Ranters were not interested in political power at all. Popular radicalism took many diverse directions in these heady days, and never showed much sign of flowing in a single river.

It would be wrong to suppose that there was no impetus to reform within the Rump itself, but it soon became blunted. Most members were shocked to discover how thoroughly unpopular their regime was; it shook their morale, and one or two committed suicide. They could not reduce the weight of taxation or disband the army by whose sufferance they sat, for the young king was preparing to use Ireland as a springboard for invasion, and the reconquest of that country was urgent. Scotland, too, proclaimed King Charles II. The Rump declared in March 1649 that it would dissolve and make way for a newly elected parliament 'so soon as may possibly stand with the safety of the people', but this was an empty promise, because safety was so slow in coming. Not only Ireland and Scotland and hostile powers on the continent threatened it, but also the sullen antagonism of the gentry of England. Any honest appeal to the people through general elections might return a parliament hostile to the very continuance of the Commonwealth. When the army put pressure on the Rump in May 1649 to make way for 'a new representative', it responded with an alternative proposal, which was to hold carefully regulated elections to the many seats that had been vacant since Pride's Purge, but to enable the active Rumpers to go on sitting indefinitely. Such a scheme was quite unacceptable to the army, and Cromwell's opposition persuaded the Rump to shelve it, but it was to crop up again at intervals over the next three years and more.

Meanwhile the Rump was so anxious to conciliate the men of substance throughout the country, whose influence would count in future elections, that it smothered those proposals for reform that would offend their conservative prejudices or cost the taxpayer money. It also wound up the hated county committees within a year or so, but it could not restore the JPs to their traditional functions without removing and replacing large numbers of them, since so many who had been parliamentarians in the wars would never condone the king's death. The fact that they took the Engagement to be faithful to the Commonwealth as it was established without a king or House of Lords, which the Rump imposed on all men over eighteen, was no guarantee of their loyalty. The hand of the central government was still heavy upon the local communities, and some counties were in effect run by local bosses whom Underdown has likened to the French Intendants (29, 31).

The army against the Rump

For two-and-a-half years the army, busy fighting as it was in Ireland and Scotland, had to swallow its discontent with the Rump's failure either to enact reforms or to make way for a successor. Cromwell himself was in Ireland from August 1649 to May 1650 and in Scotland from July 1650 to August 1651. Only after the battle of Worcester on 3 September 1651 was he free to resume his seat in parliament and his role as the army's chief spokesman.

By that time the difference of temper between the soldiers and the politicians had widened disturbingly. Officers and men who had fought through three more campaigning seasons in harsh and hostile countries were more convinced than ever that they owed their victories to the Lord's presence with them, and that it was their business to speak for not only the people of England but the people of God. The work that the Commonwealth should be about, they believed, was a godly reformation. Those two words embraced many things: the establishment of zealous preaching ministers to propagate the Gospel throughout the land; the restriction of public office to honest, God-fearing men; the reform of the law so as to make its remedies swifter, cheaper and surer and its penalties more humane; the better relief of poverty; and the improvement of social justice in various other ways. The army saw the Rumpers as worldly oligarchs, contemptuous of 'the cause of the people of God' and clinging to power for their own profit.

The parliament-men were not so generally corrupt as the army supposed, but enough of them had enriched themselves improperly through their tempting opportunities to make the charge plausible (2, 29, 42). They showed some modest reforming activity during 1650, concerning themselves with poor relief, ordering all legal proceedings to be conducted in English, and instituting local Commissions for the Propagation of the Gospel in Wales and in the north (3a, 33). Thereafter they lapsed more and more into the politics of survival. They formed caucuses and interest-groups, they ganged up (especially the lawyers among them) against proposals that they disliked, and they set their faces against any measures that might stir up the hostility of the country gentry. The group that had formerly been most concerned for social reform, in which Henry Marten and Thomas Chaloner were prominent, now interested itself mainly in promoting trade, national power and prestige. It is significant that the Navigation Act, aimed to boost English shipping and commerce in face of Dutch rivalry, was the Rump's main legislative achievement in 1651, and the commercially motivated Dutch war its chief preoccupation in 1652.

As soon as Cromwell returned from the battlefield he pressed the House to declare when it would make way for a new parliament. It tried at first to revive the scheme for holding elections only to the vacant seats, and when that proved unacceptable it voted, reluctantly and after long debate, that it would dissolve no

later than 3 November 1654. That was a full three years ahead –
nearly six years after Pride's Purge and fourteen after the last
general election. The army was naturally dissatisfied, and from
then on its discontent mounted by stages until it expelled the
Rump in April 1653. From June 1652 the Dutch war pushed
reform proposals well into the background. The war was sup-
ported enthusiastically by the dominant faction led by Sir Arthur
Haselrig and Thomas Scot, who jealously defended the Rump's
monopoly of political authority, especially against any challenge
from the army, and also by the Marten-Chaloner group. Whether
Cromwell disliked the war from the start is not clear, but he soon
came to do so. Besides dividing 'the Protestant interest' in
Europe, it cost so much that it killed all hope of reducing the unprecedented level of direct taxation or phasing out the hated
excise. The Rump had already sold off the lands of the crown and
the church; now, to make ends meet, it confiscated and offered for
sale the estates of over seven hundred royalist gentlemen in
addition to those who had lost their lands earlier. This offended
the army, not only because it deepened old divisions which Cromwell for one wanted to see healed, but because some of the victims
had surrendered upon terms that secured to them their landed
property. The army that had granted those terms felt its honour
to be at stake.

The first wave of the army's agitation culminated in a strong
petition by the Council of Officers to the Rump in August 1652.
It renewed the pressure for a new parliament, though Cromwell
used his authority to tone down its demands and stifle any actual
threat of force. The Rump responded by instructing a committee
to prepare a 'bill for a new representative', which had first been
mooted a year earlier. The committee, however, allowed the bill
to go to sleep again until the army officers started to renew their
agitation at the turn of the year. Again Cromwell damped down
his officers' militancy, striving constantly to avert an open breach,
and again the Rump, under pressure, revived the bill. This time it
put the responsible committee under the special care of Major-
General Harrison, thinking no doubt to placate the army. It was
probably unaware that Harrison had by now lost faith in elected
parliaments and aimed to put power directly into the hands of the

saints. He was in close touch with the fieriest Fifth Monarchist preacher in London, Christopher Feake, lecturer at St Anne's Blackfriars, where the crowded weekly meetings for prayer and propaganda became the focus for all the hottest millenarians in the capital.

The army officers kept up their meetings and their pressure until the bill for a new representative was given its first reading on 23 February 1653. The member who introduced it, however, was not Harrison but Haselrig, who is not recorded as ever being appointed to the drafting committee. Haselrig had been so hostile to the army's aspirations, and was to remain such a bitter enemy of Cromwell and his fellow-officers, that his apparent taking over of the bill is almost evidence enough that it was not what they would have wished. Just what was in it we cannot know, since it does not survive, but all the signs are that the officers never accepted it as a satisfactory response to their sustained pressure for a new elected parliament. Cromwell himself actually stayed away from the House from mid-March to mid-April, and so boycotted several of the weekly debates on it.

Yet the bill did not, as generations of historians have supposed, order elections only to the vacant seats, leaving the Rumpers to sit on indefinitely. Dr Worden has demonstrated beyond reasonable doubt that it provided for the Rump's final dissolution and the meeting of a new parliament in the following November, with the seats redistributed on lines similar to what the officers had agreed in the amended Agreement of the People in 1649 (42, 43). Why, then, did Cromwell so precipitately dissolve the Rump on 20 April? The answer is far from certain, but some facts are clear.

Cromwell plainly did not want the bill to pass in the form in which it stood around mid-April. For that reason he called a meeting on the evening of 19 April between about twenty leading MPs and some senior officers, and put to them a startling alternative. To save the Commonwealth from its present divisions, he proposed that the Rump should hand over the supreme authority for a while to about forty 'men fearing God, and of approved integrity', nominated by itself, and should then dissolve itself. This interim government was to hold the reins, with sufficient authority to institute the reforms so long desired, until it judged the nation to be settled enough to elect its own representatives to govern it once more. At the end of the meeting he thought he had got a sufficient number of MPs to agree that the Rump would not proceed further with its bill, whose progress had been leisurely so far, until it had fully considered his alternative scheme.

Next morning he stayed at Whitehall, polishing up the details of his proposal with a few trusted counsellors. He would not believe it when a messenger reported that the Rump was not only debating the bill again, but trying to rush it through that very morning. After a third such message, however, he hastened to the House and found it to be true. Having listened in growing anger, he rose and denounced the members in blistering terms, then called in a file of musketeers to turn them out. The bill itself he stuffed under his cloak, and it is hard to say which are the more suspicious facts: that he never let it be seen again, and changed his opinions about it in subsequent speeches, or that the Rumpers never publicly defended it while he lived and were still coy about its contents even after he was dead.

One possible explanation of his violent act, to which Worden inclines, is that he had ceased to want an elected parliament at all, because he had become converted to the same Fifth Monarchist convictions as Harrison, namely that the time had come to entrust the government to a body of hand-picked saints, dedicated to inaugurating the kingdom of Christ. There are difficulties about this hypothesis. There is evidence that Cromwell and Harrison in fact regarded each other rather warily at this time. Cromwell had to all appearances been at one with the Council of Officers in pressing for a newly elected parliament until well into 1653. Furthermore, he evidently had no alternative plan to execute after he expelled the Rump; he clearly did not know what to do next. The nominated assembly ('Barebone's Parliament') which he eventually summoned was a different sort of body from the care-taker government that he proposed on 19 April, and he conceived it not as a superior alternative to an elected parliament but as a temporary substitute for one. In this writer's view he never shared the belief that the people as a whole should lose their suf-frages or that the saints alone were called by Christ to govern (37; cf. 42).

It seems simpler to suppose that the key to Cromwell's action lies in the bill itself, or in what he thought was in the bill, since he found it so urgent to prevent it from passing. He apparently continued to believe that there was some devious way in which the Rumpers could have made use of it to perpetuate their power, even though it was not the simple sort of 'recruiter' bill that historians until recently supposed. Two hypotheses about what it may have contained – or omitted – to rouse his suspicions have been put forward, but inevitably they contain a good deal of speculation and they are too complex to summarize here (37). He certainly believed that the bill did not define the qualifications for future MPs strictly enough to prevent a majority being chosen who would want to bring the monarchy back, and that the Rump was making no adequate provision to ensure that the qualifications, such as they were, would be enforced.

That may be sufficient to explain why he dissolved it. He knew that general elections were bound to be a risk, and that the transition from the old parliament to a fresh one would need close supervision, to ensure that the Commonwealth's new governors could be trusted to keep their Engagement to be faithful to it. Whoever scrutinized the election returns, the army's co-operation might well be needed to ensure that men who were seriously disaffected to the Commonwealth were kept out. The hazard was acceptable and the achievement of a new parliament desirable so long as the Rump and the army could watch over the transfer of authority in mutual trust and harmony, but the worsening relations between them in March and April made the risk too high. That the Rump tried to rush its bill through because it feared a military *coup* is understandable, but so is the army's suspicion that Haselrig's now dominant faction was still trying to trick it. The Rump only existed because the army had done its bidding in Pride's Purge, so why, the officers could ask, should they be denied any participation in the long-delayed transmission of power to a new parliament? There were rumours abroad just before the dissolution that the Rump intended to remove Cromwell from the generalship and remodel the whole command of the army. These rumours may have been unfounded, but it is significant that they circulated, and were found credible.

Barebone's Parliament

By expelling the Rump, Cromwell closed the option of calling a newly elected parliament for some time to come. Not only had he no legal right to summon one, especially since the Long Parliament could not be dissolved without its own consent, but even if he had made the attempt, the men likeliest to be chosen would have been either Presbyterians of the kind excluded by Pride's Purge, or crypto-royalists, or republican sympathizers with the Rump. All these would have been sharply hostile to the army and its aspirations.

Another option was a military dictatorship, and there were indeed some voices urging Cromwell to take upon himself the role of a second Moses. But it was far from his thoughts or desires, and he cast the burden of decision onto the Council of Officers, in which there were two main factions. One was led by Major-General John Lambert, young, brave, impetuous, ambitious, and angry with the Rump because it had abolished the office of Lord Deputy of Ireland just as he was about to take it up. He was not given to millenarian visions; what moved him was the sort of distrust that clever young generals, fresh from active service, often feel towards prevaricating, self-interested politicians. He argued in favour of entrusting the government to a small council of ten or twelve men, presumably with the idea of bringing parliament back into a legislative role when the country was settled enough to elect one again. From late in April civil affairs were in fact put in the care of a small provisional Council of State under Lambert's presidency, and he was enjoying his new dignity. The other faction in the Council of Officers was headed by Harrison, for whom the only real question was how best to fulfil Daniel's prophecy and commit supreme power to the saints; he currently favoured a sanhedrin of seventy godly men, after the biblical example of Israel. Cromwell too favoured a larger body, though for somewhat different reasons, and he later took credit for proposing 140, the number eventually agreed on. Although it would have to be nominated rather than elected, a body of that size could be made to look broadly representative of regional interests, and could more plausibly enact the first instalments of a godly reformation. So each English county was allotted a number of members roughly corresponding to its size and wealth, while Wales and Ireland got six apiece and Scotland five.

The notion that Cromwell was temporarily converted to Fifth Monarchist ideals used to rest partly on a mistake about the way in which this nominated assembly was chosen. The story usually told is that Cromwell and the Council of Officers sent circular letters to the Independent congregations or 'gathered churches' in every county, inviting them to name men fit to rule a godly commonwealth, and then selected the members mainly from the lists that were returned. In fact no such invitation was sent out, though some particular officers consulted particular ministers whom they trusted. Certain churches in at least six counties and two individual towns did send in recommendations, but they did so unbidden. Some of their nominees were summoned, some were passed over; only fifteen members are known to have been named by the churches. The Council of Officers in fact chose whom it pleased; any officer could propose a candidate, and a simple majority vote decided whether he was called. Cromwell later asserted that there was 'not an officer of the degree of a captain but named more than he himself did'. But the officers observed an important restraint, probably on Cromwell's advice and against Harrison's inclinations: they did not nominate each other. Apart from a very few garrison commanders and Admirals Blake and Monck, Barebone's Parliament contained practically no serving officers (37, 39).

Two different kinds of expectation lay behind the summoning of this assembly, both among those who chose it and among those who were chosen. Cromwell and the majority of the nominated members regarded it as a temporary substitute for an elected parliament, performing similar functions and filling a gap until the country could return to the real thing. Harrison's faction in the army and the minority of millenarian zealots in the assembly, by contrast, saw it as the inauguration of a totally new order. Parliaments in their view were mere 'carnal' institutions, and God had set them aside along with kings; they could derive no authority from the people, for the people had none to confer. Power stemmed only from Christ, and He bestowed it only on His chosen saints.

This is not to deny that Cromwell too looked forward to the realization of Christ's kingdom on earth and hoped for wonderful things from this new government. He opened it on 4 July with a speech of visionary enthusiasm, trusting that its meeting would prove to be 'a day of the power of Christ' – a stage, that is, on the road towards that cherished goal. But his expectation was that Christ would reign 'in our hearts', not through the sort of crude physical dictatorship envisaged by the Fifth Monarchists. Even in his opening speech he expressly looked forward to the time when the people would be fit to exercise their suffrages again. He enjoined the assembly to sit no longer than 4 November 1654 and to hand over to another body, nominated by itself, which was 'to take care for a succession in government' and to sit no longer than a year. The implication is that he contemplated a return to a constitutional settlement that would include regular elected parliaments by about the end of 1655.

The assembly decided to meet in the Commons' House and to call itself a parliament. It elected a Speaker, sent for the mace which Cromwell had impounded in April, and in most other ways followed the time-honoured procedures of the House of Commons. It was by no means the collection of ignorant, fanatical nobodies that its royalist detractors pretended. Five-sixths of the members ranked as gentlemen, and though the proportion of lesser gentry was much higher than in normal parliaments they did include a viscount, a baron, four baronets and four knights. Even Praise-God Barebone, whose name was soon contemptuously attached to the parliament and who was one of the two dozen undoubted plebeians in it, was a City merchant of some substance. No fewer than a hundred and nineteen members were JPs, and though some were new to the bench, eighty-nine of them had sat on it in 1650 or earlier. Well over forty had been to a university, and about as many to an inn of court. Although only twenty-four had sat in any previous parliament, sixty-seven were elected to subsequent ones and six sat in the post-Restoration House of Lords. Neither in education nor in social status were the members collectively inadequate for their appointed role, and most of them had at least some local administrative experience.

What eventually brought Barebone's Parliament to an end was a division within its own ranks. It did not appear too serious at first. The members set about an ambitious programme of reforming legislation with real enthusiasm, and by working much harder than the Rump they made considerable progress with it. But though they could work together on many matters in reasonable harmony, there were certain issues which from early on caused them to polarize between a moderate wing and a radical one; these were never so distinct as parties, but roughly corresponded to the two divergent views of what their function really was. The moderate majority wanted to carry on the work of a reforming parliament within the broad framework of the historic laws and customs of England, but the radicals were eager in varying degrees to make a clean sweep, so as to clear the site for the New Jerusalem. Only a dozen were professed Fifth Monarchy men, but between forty and fifty members took a radical line on most of the controversial issues, and very occasionally they could attract enough allies to muster nearly sixty votes.

The most contentious issues involved religion, the law and property; sometimes all three at once. The first to appear concerned tithes. Many moderates agreed in desiring some means of maintaining public preachers that would be fairer in itself and less burdensome to sectarian consciences, yet tithes were legal property, whether of the clergy whose livings were based on them or of lay owners who had acquired 'impropriate' tithes since the Reformation. Moreover the extreme radicals wanted to abolish a publicly maintained ministry altogether. Similar difficulties arose over the rights of lay patrons to present ministers to parish livings. These advowsons, as such rights were called, were so often abused that some moderates were ready with the radicals to abolish them, but advowsons were also pieces of property, and marketable. The reform of the law was another great bone of contention. The common law was a living growth, and there was a great difference between the moderates' desire to cut off its dead wood and extend its benefits and the declared aim of the radicals to jettison the whole venerable organism in favour of a simple written code. So much of the law was concerned with property; lay the axe to the one, it was felt, and the other was in jeopardy. But religion was to provoke the final and fatal division.

Fewer and fewer members attended the House as the autumn wore on, probably because many had lost faith in it as a responsible government and an instrument of reform. Cromwell was reported as saying that he was 'more troubled now with the fool than before with the knave'. He was hampered in his efforts to negotiate peace terms with the Dutch, which reached a critical stage in November and early December, because Harrison and the Fifth Monarchist firebrands at Blackfriars and their allies in the House were stridently opposing any peace at all. The preachers railed against Cromwell himself, calling him the Great Beast 'and many other Scripture ill names'. They had crazy visions of a career of conquest, begun already by England's saints against the wealth-corrupted merchants of Holland and destined to end only with the defeat of Antichrist in Rome itself. Within the House the behaviour of the hotter millenarians became hard for the moderates to bear. They would come in from their prayer-meetings, ostentatiously carrying their bibles and claiming to speak in the power of the Spirit; one, for instance, claimed that 'he spake it not, but the Lord in him'.

Yet when the moderates turned up in strength to elect a new Council of State on 1 November they won a landslide victory, which left only four radicals among thirty-one councillors. But they did not follow it up, and some of them were probably waiting already for a pretext to bring Barebone's Parliament to an end. They needed some alternative government to take its place, however, and the man who supplied it was Lambert. He had withdrawn from politics when the parliament had met, probably in disgust, and home in his native Yorkshire had drafted a written constitution, with Cromwell cast in the role of a constitutional monarch. The council sent for him in November to sound him out about taking over the command in Scotland, where a royalist rising in the Highlands was escalating. He did not want the job, but he discussed his scheme with a few fellow officers, and together they put it to Cromwell himself. They found him interested in their constitution, but adamantly opposed to both the royal title and any idea of another military *coup*.

29

But what if Barebone's Parliament dissolved itself? The opportunity presented itself early in December when the House debated a long-awaited set of proposals for settling who should hold parish livings. A body of commissioners was proposed who, dividing the country into circuits, would have power to eject all unworthy ministers and to approve all who were newly presented to benefices. For six days this was intensely debated, only to be defeated by fifty-six votes to fifty-four on the first and crucial clause. It seems that the radical sectaries who opposed any publicly maintained clergy on principle were joined by others who thought that this scheme was not the best means to the desired end.

That vote was taken on Saturday 10 December. On the Sunday the moderate leaders laid their plans, probably in concert with Lambert. They got to the House early on Monday morning and rose one after another to denounce the radicals for threatening the law, the ministry, the army, and even property itself. They then marched out with the Speaker before them – he was obviously in the plot – and processed to Whitehall Palace, where they resigned their authority back into Cromwell's hands. Within hours a clear majority of members had signed a brief document of abdication (39).

The Protectorate established

Cromwell now had little choice but to take on the headship of the state. He had a strong sense that anarchy would have ensued if he had declined: 'I saw we were running headlong into confusion and disorder,' he said later, 'and would necessarily run into blood.' Lambert and the Council of Officers naturally pressed the Instrument of Government on him again, and this time he accepted it, though with the title of Lord Protector instead of king. After intense discussions with his officers, to perfect the details and select his original council, he was solemnly installed in his new office in Westminster Hall, where he swore to govern wholly according to the rules of the new constitution and the laws of the land. Only four days had passed since Barebone's Parliament resigned.

Occasionally, though less often nowadays, one still finds the Protectorate glibly branded as a military dictatorship, but, except in the very limited sense that Cromwell would not have become head of state if he had not been general of an army, the description is most misleading. He himself praised the constitution because 'it limited me and bound my hands to act nothing to the prejudice of the nations without consent of a council [and] parliament'. He valued it because it separated the legislative and executive powers, instead of leaving both under the control of a parliament that acknowledged no bounds to its authority, and because it restored the old idea of a balance in the constitution. Protector, council and parliament obviously had some correspondence to king, privy council and parliament under the monarchy, but each element differed so much in constitution and powers that this was not a mere return to old forms under new management.

The executive power was vested in the Protector and the council, and he was bound, as kings had not been bound, to govern in all things by its advice. Nor was he free, as kings had been, to appoint or dismiss councillors at his pleasure. This restraint would have meant little if the council had been an obedient rubber stamp or a junto of army officers, but it was neither. Its role in decision-making has often been underestimated and the military element in it exaggerated. Only four of Cromwell's fifteen original councillors (Lambert, Fleetwood, Desborough, Skippon) belonged to the field army; Sydenham was governor of the Isle of Wight, but Colonel Philip Jones had long ago become an administrator rather than a soldier and Colonel Edward Montagu's army days were well in the past. Civilians outnumbered soldiers by two to one, and their preponderance increased with the subsequent appointments to the council.

Just as executive authority belonged to the Protector and council, the legislative was vested in the Protector and parliament, but here his role was even more circumscribed. He was bound to call parliament at least every three years and to keep it sitting for at least five months. If it passed any bill to which he objected, he could withhold his consent for twenty days, but thereafter parliament could insist that it became law provided (and it was a big proviso) that it contained nothing contrary to the Instrument itself. But that did not mean, as is often stated, that there was no way of changing the constitution. He made it clear in a major speech on 12 September 1654 that except in its most fundamental features the Instrument's provisions were negotiable; it could simply not be altered unilaterally by either parliament or Protector.

Parliament itself was reformed in the way that the army had been demanding since 1647, though the precise distribution of seats was as the Rump's bill for a new representative had defined it, apart from the addition of thirty members apiece for Scotland and Ireland. Scores of small boroughs lost their seats, and the proportion of county representatives was raised from less than a fifth (in 1640) to about two-thirds. The franchise also followed the Rump's bill, and gave the vote in the counties to all adult males who owned real or personal property worth £200. It did not have to be freehold property, as under the monarchy, or landed property at all. If one is to compare it with the old forty-shilling freehold qualification, fixed in 1430 when money had been worth vastly more, £200 was reckoned as equivalent to about £10 per year.

In one important area the Instrument gave more to the Protector than the monarchy had enjoyed. It stipulated that he should have enough revenue for any army of 30,000 men (slightly more than half its actual strength in 1653) and a sufficient fleet, with in addition £200,000 per year for the civil government. Parliament's control over taxation began only after these basic needs had been met, though how they were to be met and at whose discretion was left undefined. This was one of the undoubted weaknesses in the Instrument. Another lay in the complex procedures for removing unsatisfactory councillors and appointing new ones, and still more in the assumption that councillors should serve for life unless they were convicted of corruption or other grave offences. But on the whole the Instrument was an honest piece of constitution-building. It was not so much a turning back from some radical alternative Commonwealth, which however theoretically desirable had never been formulated in practicable terms, as an attempt to put into practice the principles which Ireton had framed and the Army Council had endorsed in the Heads of the Proposals in 1647, with modifications arising from lessons learnt in the intervening years. Its fatal weakness lay not in its content but in its origin. What right had any small group of army officers to impose any constitution at all? Any elected parliament was bound to ask that question.

Meanwhile the Instrument gave Cromwell and the council the authority to make ordinances until the first parliament of the new regime met in September 1654, though they were to be subject to parliamentary confirmation. Cromwell used this temporary power boldly but responsibly, and nowhere more so than in the settlement of religion (3b, c). Nothing had so far replaced the Presbyterian establishment of the later 1640s, which was crumbling away even in most of those limited regions where it had ever got off the ground. The Instrument had laid down that there should be a public profession of the Christian faith, to set the guidelines for belief and worship in the parish churches, but that all protestant Christians who dissented from this profession should be free to associate and worship in their own way. It did not, however, prescribe how candidates for parish livings were to be adjudged fit for them, or how unworthy ministers were to be removed. The Rump had long evaded the problem, and Barebone's Parliament had split irreparably over it. Two Cromwellian ordinances grasped the nettle. The first, in March 1654, set up a central body of 'commissioners for approbation of ministers', generally called the Triers, who had to approve the candidates whom patrons presented to livings. They included Presbyterians, Independents and Baptists; twenty-three ministers and ten laymen. They imposed no rigid doctrinal tests; they had simply to satisfy themselves that ministers-to-be were well grounded in the Christian faith, decent in their moral lives and capable of preaching. The other ordinance, in August, set up local commissioners in the counties, the Ejectors, to weed out ministers who were drunken, immoral, grossly ignorant or negligent.

What developed from this settlement was a broad established church which probably embraced a greater proportion of the laity and clergy than the Church of England had ever done since the Reformation, and which certainly extended a broader toleration outside it than until much later times. In contrast with pre-war and post-Restoration times, no Englishman was subject to the coercive jurisdiction of any ecclesiastical court, though many submitted voluntarily to the 'godly discipline' of their own churches. Cromwell's toleration extended to the Jews, whom he readmitted to England in 1656 despite considerable opposition within his council. Even the Roman Catholic community, or a strong section of it, sought Cromwell's recognition and toleration, and though that was not practical politics they lived in relative quiet and their spokesman, the royalist Sir Kenelm Digby, enjoyed Cromwell's favour and friendship (5, 21). Only those whose religious views led them to conspire against the state or to break the laws or to interrupt the worship of others had anything to fear under the Protectorate, and Cromwell intervened more than once to mitigate the persecution to which many local magistrates subjected the Quakers.

Some historians, notably Christopher Hill (11), have characterized the whole Protectorate as a phase of conservative reaction which set England well on the road to the restoration of the monarchy. It is true that Cromwell had set his face against radical movements, whether Leveller or Fifth Monarchist, which threatened the time-honoured fabric of law and property and social hierarchy. It is also true that he restored the authority of the Exchequer in the financial sphere and made a partial return to older institutions in some other branches of the administration. His own Household was loosely modelled on the royal one, though on a far more modest scale. But, with regard not only to national administration but to the character of the regime as a whole, Professor Aylmer suggests that the key-note was not so much conservative reaction as 'the long-delayed and grossly overdue return to normality after the protracted but essentially temporary expedients of a wartime and then post-war regime' (2).

It can plausibly be argued that Cromwell and his council retained more of a reforming spirit than the Rump had displayed. If his hopes of a godly reformation remained only very partially fulfilled, that was mainly because his parliaments did not share them. When the Protectorate did become unmistakably more conservative in tone, as it did from about 1657 onwards, it was due as we shall see to a combination of a new breed of civilian

34

Cromwellians, a new parliamentary constitution, and his own diminishing vitality. Though he sought from the start to recover the support of the gentry and other men of substance, he did so not as the Rump had done, by a play-safe avoidance of provocation, but by more positive means: by seeking (at least initially) to bury old differences between royalists and parliamentarians and between Presbyterians and Independents, by ending the Dutch war and consequently reducing taxation, and by striking anew that Elizabethan chord which had linked together protestantism, patriotism and national pride. He did not court the gentry, the lawyers and other conservative-interest groups by abandoning the causes he believed in: propagating the gospel, liberty of conscience, a 'reformation of manners' (in the sense of raising standards of moral conduct), the reform of the law and the improvement of social justice. Had he done so his path might have been smoother.

Cromwell and the nation

Cromwell said he longed for 'a government by consent', but asked how consent could be found when the divisions in the nation were so many and so deep. He won over a few royalists and rather more of the old political Presbyterians, but most remained hostile. He never reconciled the parliamentary republicans such as Haselrig, Bradshaw, Vane, Marten and Ludlow. There were 'commonwealthsmen' too in the army, and he had to cashier a number of old comrades who publicly challenged his authority as Protector or worked to undermine it. Harrison also had to go, for he and other militant Fifth Monarchists incited their brethren to armed resistance; when he and his ally John Carew and others were summoned before the council for it, Carew told Cromwell to his face that when he took over from Barebone's Parliament he 'took the crown off from the head of Christ and put it upon his own'. The Levellers, though broken as an organized movement, had left a residue of frustrated democratic aspiration which erupted again in large demonstrations of sympathy when Lilburne returned home to challenge his banishment and stood his last trial in August 1653. In a nation torn by so many recent divisions

35

government by consensus was scarcely possible. If a free plebiscite could have been held it would probably have brought back Charles II, but that would not have mended the divisions or solved the political problems that civil war had failed to solve. The Restoration would only revive a degree of national unity, and a very imperfect degree at that, when the English Revolution had collapsed from within.

One problem which the Protectorate faced, and which had greatly increased the unpopularity both of Charles I's personal rule and of the Long Parliament, was that of making the local communities comply with the commands of the central government. Cromwell tried at first to relax governmental pressure and to place more trust in the gentry who regarded themselves as the natural governors of their counties, and to some extent they responded (8e). But the parliament that met in September 1654 gave him a chilling setback. It was not just the presence of a few crypto-royalists and rather larger numbers of political Presbyterians and Rumper republicans that made it unmanageable, though the republicans did their best. Probably the largest group of members was the unaligned country gentlemen who had an inbuilt distrust of 'swordsmen' and central authority, and Haselrig and his allies promptly led them in questioning the validity of the Instrument's restraints upon the power of parliament. Cromwell intervened after eight days and pointed out that a formal acknowledgement of the new constitution had been written into every member's election return; both electors and elected, he claimed, were bound by it. The members were not allowed to resume their seats unless they signed a promise that they would not attempt 'to alter the government, as it is settled in one single person and a parliament'. That got rid of the doctrinaire republicans, but those who signed still wanted to know why a few army officers should lay down the laws of the constitution rather than themselves, the people's elected representatives. So instead of confirming the many ordinances made by the Protector and council, regularizing the government's finances and carrying on the work of reformation as Cromwell had hoped, they spent all their time rewriting the constitution according to their own notions. He might have gone far to meet a constitution that carried the stamp of parliamentary approval, as he did in 1657, but this one contravened certain principles which he had declared to be fundamental. It drastically altered the balance between the council and the parliament; it permitted parliament to legislate on matters that would seriously limit religious liberty, without his consent; and it envisaged a large reduction of the army, just when a royalist rising in the Highlands had lately been suppressed and a potentially more serious one was known to be brewing in England. Rather than face a confrontation over these sensitive issues, on which he could not yield, he dissolved parliament on 22 January 1655. It had not passed a single bill or voted a single penny in taxes.

The expected royalist insurrection broke out in March, but good intelligence and vigorous counter-measures confined it to one region. Penruddock's Rising, as it was called, broke out in Wiltshire and was hunted down to defeat in Devon. It could have been much more serious, and the punishment of its participants was very moderate indeed compared with what was meted out to the rebels in 1569 and 1685 (30). But to complete its suppression that reliable soldier John Desborough was made Major-General of the south-western counties, and in the autumn Cromwell extended the same expedient to the rest of England. One purpose was to reduce taxation. He had already reduced the main direct tax, the monthly assessment, from £120,000 to £90,000; now he cut it further to £60,000, making the savings by considerably reducing the standing army. To provide security against any further royalist conspiracies he raised a local mounted militia, dividing England into eleven (later twelve) regions for the purpose and setting a major-general over each. The primary role of the major-generals was to co-ordinate the command of the local militia and of any units of the field army in their regions, and to keep a check on the movements of known royalists. To pay for the militia the major-generals levied a tax of 10 per cent on the landed income of all royalists with estates worth £100 a year or more. This was very rough justice, not only because it had no parliamentary sanction, but because only a small proportion of royalists had engaged in conspiracy against the Protectorate.

But Cromwell was not content to use the major-generals solely for the purpose of local defence and security. He instructed them by 'their constant carriage and conversation [to] encourage and promote godliness and virtue, and discourage and discountenance all profaneness and ungodliness', and they were to do this by prodding the local JPs into enforcing the existing laws against drunkenness, immorality, swearing, blaspheming and sabbath-breaking. The major-generals did not supersede the existing local authorities, but they leaned heavily on them, and that was the major cause of their unpopularity – that upstart swordsmen should presume to tell the gentry magistrates, the 'natural' rulers of their county communities, how to go about their business. Naturally they were also disliked for their attempts to bring the power of the state – especially its military power – to bear on imposing an oppressive puritan moral code, but the zeal with which they did this varied much from one to another. Their un-popularity was probably greatest with those who were already irreconcilable with the Protectorate, the royalists and the re-publicans (3e, 25, 26).

A new constitution

Cromwell called a new parliament in September 1656, a year earlier than he was obliged to under the Instrument. He claimed that this was against his better judgement, but that he bowed to pressure from the army officers. Nevertheless his financial needs were great, because the unprovoked attacks which he had launched against the Spanish colonies, and especially his capture of Jamaica in May 1655, had inevitably driven Spain into declaring war, and it was proving expensive. The major-generals were con-fident that they could influence the elections sufficiently to secure a compliant parliament, but they were proved wrong, and the council over-reacted by abusing its power under the Instrument to check that the members were qualified. It debarred over a hundred of them from taking their seats. This, then, was a purged parliament from the start, but it did in time put the Protectorate and its revenues on a more legal footing and it produced quite a useful crop of legislation.

Even though known opponents of the regime were excluded,

those who did sit proceeded to group themselves in a most significant way. In opposition to the army officers and others who were initially identified with the Protectorate, a new party of Cromwellian supporters emerged, conservative but not royalist, mainly civilian but including such proven servicemen as General Monck and Edward Montagu, now General at Sea. Some of its leaders were younger men with a royalist background, notably Lord Broghill, Sir Charles Wolseley and Viscount Fauconberg, who married one of Cromwell's daughters. It was particularly strong in lawyer-politicians like Nathaniel Fiennes, Bulstrode Whitelocke, Sir Thomas Widdington, John Glyn and William Lenthall, men whose natural conservatism did not inhibit them from seeing a promising future if they could remould the Protectorate to suit their own political style. These 'new Cromwellians', who drew in quite a number of the old political families, stood for constitutional government, for upholding the old laws of the land, for shifting the basis of the regime still further from military to civilian foundations, and for restoring local administration to the 'natural' rulers of the counties, the leading gentry.

Two issues made this new line of division dramatically clear. One was the legality of the system of major-generals, which Major-General Desborough raised by introducing a bill to regularize the Decimation tax which paid for it. After intense debate the bill was heavily defeated on 29 January 1657. Cromwell acquiesced in parliament's decision, though he frankly regretted it, and the major-generals' regime was rapidly wound down. Thereafter he resumed his attempt to win the broad support of the political nation, but the 'swordsmen' had caused a serious setback to the Protectorate's limited popularity and not much time was left for it to strike fresh roots (3e).

The other great issue was a new constituion. From the new conservative Cromwellians' point of view there were two main defects in the present one. The first, emphasized by Cromwell's indifferent health, concerned his successor, who according to the Instrument was to be elected by the council. They must have feared that it would choose another army man – his son-in-law Fleetwood, perhaps, or the ambitious Lambert. The second lay in the fact that it had so far proved impossible to secure co-operative parliaments without arbitrarily excluding large numbers of members, and even then their co-operation was unpredictable. Consequently the same civilian party that had rejected the major-generals concocted a new written constitution which they introduced in parliament in February and presented to Cromwell at the end of March, under the name of the Humble Petition and Advice. It tackled the first problem by requesting Cromwell to assume the crown, partly because it would give his regime an aura of legality, partly because his guileless son Richard was a more acceptable successor than any army grandee. Its solution to the second problem was a new upper house of parliament, with members appointed by the Protector for life, so as to entrench his loyalest supporters in a position from which they could act as a check on the Commons. To end arbitrary exclusions, it laid down that members could only be debarred from either House by the decision of the House itself.

The snag was that Cromwell was asked to accept or reject the whole package; he could not agree to some provisions and refuse others. He was greatly attracted by a constitution which emanated from a parliament, even a purged one, rather than from a junto of army officers, and he liked many things in it including the 'Other House'. But he had strong qualms about becoming king, and the army showed its opposition from the start. There were many weeks of negotiation before he finally refused the crown, and he seems to have been in two minds until almost the end. His decision is often attributed to the army's unrest, and particularly to the concerted refusal of Lambert, Fleetwood and Desborough to serve him any longer if he should accept. But the latter may have been little more than the last touch that tipped the scales, and the reasons that he himself gave probably weighed more heavily with him. They were first that he would have offended thousands who had fought the Lord's battles with him, and who would have thought that King Oliver was betraying their common cause, and secondly that he himself had a sense that God had pronounced against the title as well as the house of Stuart. 'I would not seek to set up that that providence hath destroyed and laid in the dust,' he said, 'and I would not build

Jericho again.' But despite his refusal, parliament did decide (by three votes) to let him accept the Humble Petition as the Commonwealth's new constitution without changing his title, and he was solemnly reinstalled as Lord Protector on 26 June 1657.

This was a long step towards founding his government on law and consent, but there were some prices to pay. The Humble Petition slightly narrowed the range of religious toleration, and though the practical effect upon radical puritans was probably negligible while he lived, their allegiance to the Protectorate was weakened. Lambert was stripped of his commissions and pensioned off, because of his dubious loyalty and his over-eager interest in the succession. But real trouble only blew up when parliament reassembled in January 1658. Now that MPs could only be kept out by a vote of the Commons, the formerly excluded republicans returned in strength, and led by Haselrig they launched a full-throated attack on the Other House. Since that is where many of Cromwell's ablest supporters now sat, his opponents had it much their own way. They were helped by, if they did not instigate, a dangerous mass petition of London citizens whose real aim was the re-establishment of the republic. Since it also aimed at subverting the army, Cromwell hastily dissolved the parliament before it could be presented. The session had lasted a mere fortnight.

It was a deeply disappointing start to the new Protectorate, but the picture was not all black. The army returned to its normal loyalty and discipline after only six officers, none of high rank, had been cashiered. The royalists' plans for a new rising were unmasked in the spring with devastating efficiency. The country was benefitting by years of internal peace and had experienced a welcome period of economic prosperity since Cromwell took office, though unfortunately a new depression was on the way. He had lately established at Durham the first English university college outside Oxford and Cambridge. Although Cromwellian rule only deepened Ireland's tragedy, the Scottish union was working rather well, and many Scots were to recall it nostalgically under the later Stuarts (4, 8). English arms won respect on the continent, for the first time in generations; they helped to acquire Dunkirk just a century after Mary Tudor lost Calais. England in fact stood higher by 1658 among the powers of Europe than at any time since the Hundred Years' War. Yet the Protectorate was marking time now, for Cromwell's vitality was ebbing, and on 3 September, the anniversary of Dunbar and Worcester, he died.

Richard Cromwell's Protectorate

Richard Cromwell was not as dim-witted or spiritless as hostile critics painted him, but he would have had to be exceptionally able to take up his father's difficult legacy with success, and that he was not. He was an ordinary, decent country squire. There have been doubts whether Oliver ever nominated him and suggestions that he might have chosen better, but the doubts are almost certainly unfounded, and any other candidate would have been open to serious objections (40). Richard had little to fear from the now demoralized royalists, and the country greeted his peaceful accession with some show of pleasure. His fatal weakness was that he lacked standing with the army, for he had never fought with it, and Fleetwood (his brother-in-law) and Desborough (his uncle by marriage) were not prepared to bow to him. Sensing their jealousy, he relied for advice mainly on his civilian councillors and on friends outside the council of a still more conservative hue. The moderate, traditionalist trend of his government endeared it to the political nation, but antagonized the army and the more radical Independents and sectaries. The officers started agitating for a commander-in-chief distinct from the Protector, which suggested a dangerous disinclination to accept the civil state as their master.

These differences were smoothed over until a new parliament met in January 1659. The republicans reappeared in some strength — they could not be excluded now — and they tried again to mobilize opposition to the whole Protectoral constitution. This time, however, they failed. They could not shake the ordinary, non-party country gentry who made up the bulk of the Commons out of recognizing Richard as Protector and the Other House as an integral part of parliament; indeed the Commons now wanted to make the latter more like the House of Lords by bringing back the faithful parliamentarian peers. That petition of the London citizens which had so alarmed Cromwell a year earlier was revived and actually presented, but, though the republicans spoke up for it one after another, the House voted by a massive majority not to thank the petitioners and gave them a cold answer.

Beaten in division after division, the republicans turned to sowing discontent in the army and among the sects. The army offered fertile ground, since scores of the junior and middle-ranking officers felt that the hopes and ideals of their years of victory had not been realized and that a gulf had opened up between themselves and the military grandees who sat on the council and in the Other House. From the winter through the spring a massive campaign of pamphlets and sermons, partly spontaneous but also fanned by the republicans, inflamed a hazy notion that 'the Good Old Cause' was being betrayed. The anonymous pamphleteers never spelt out what the Good Old Cause had been, but they evoked a powerful nostalgia for a largely mythical time when the victors in the wars had been united in purpose. They depicted the Protectorate as an apostasy, and accused the present government and parliament of leading the country back into the old monarchical tyranny. They appealed to all radical puritans by alleging that the Lord had withdrawn his presence from England since her leaders had taken to pursuing power rather than godly reformation, and to millenarians in particular by denouncing the current regime as an embodiment of the Beast, standing athwart the road forward to the kingdom of Christ (41).

Fleetwood, Desborough and the other senior officers ought to have nipped the army's unrest in the bud, but they partly shared it. Whereas Oliver had kept some sort of a balance between his older military counsellors and his newer civilian ones, even when leaning towards the latter, Richard was impelled by the former's dangerous ambitions to trust only his friends. The rift in the council widened, and Richard was reputed to be getting guidance outside it from William Pierrepont, Oliver St John and the Lords Broghill and Fauconberg, all of whom were hostile to the army. Fleetwood, Desborough and the other military grandees felt themselves denied the political influence that they thought they deserved, and at the same time distrusted by their own subordinate officers because of their association with a 'backsliding'

Court. Their position was uncomfortable, but it did not justify them in what they did at about the end of March. They then began to seek a secret *rapprochement* with the leading republican politicians such as Haselrig and Vane who, with Lambert now their active ally, were attacking the Protectorate in parliament.

This move was treachery, and it proved fatal, not only to Richard and to themselves, but eventually to the whole Commonwealth. The army chiefs bullied Richard into letting them revive the General Council of Officers, which set itself on collision course with the parliament. The latter tried to dissolve it, whereupon Fleetwood and Desborough executed a military *coup d'état* which forced Richard on 22 April to dissolve parliament instead. They had no intention then of deposing him, but they found themselves quite unable to do what they had intended, which was to keep him as a puppet Protector with themselves and their new allies (if allies they were) pulling the strings. The republicans were determined not to share power with him or even, any more than they could help, with the army commanders. The majority of their own officers, especially the junior ones, had developed so strong a revulsion against the Protectorate that they wanted it abolished and the Rump recalled to the supreme authority; the propagandists had succeeded in identifying the Good Old Cause with the good old parliament. The army grandees could not even exact any conditions from the spokesmen of the Rump, which returned to power on 7 May. Bowing to the inevitable, Richard resigned the Protectorship (which the Rump of course did not recognize) soon afterwards (3f, 7, 38, 41).

The restored Commonwealth and its collapse

The proclamation of Charles II as king lay just a year ahead, but few would have predicted so rapid a transformation. So fast did events move from now on that only a few salient developments can be spotlit here.

The 'good old parliament' was certainly old, but it had learnt nothing. It proceeded recklessly to alienate the army that had restored it in a variety of ways, especially by refusing to consider any form of power-sharing, now that the Other House had ceased to be, and by whittling away Fleetwood's grudgingly conceded authority as commander-in-chief. Only the knowledge that a new royalist rising was imminent kept the army and the Rump from quarreling openly during the summer.

The rising was timed for 1 August, but caution among the twice-burnt cavaliers coupled with good counter-intelligence confined it to the area of Cheshire and south Lancashire. There Sir George Booth got a few thousand men under arms, but they stood no chance when Lambert reached the scene and routed them. Although a real attempt had been made to ally royalists and political Presbyterians (of whom Booth was one) in the enterprise, which did not at first proclaim the king, the support for it was meagre and half-hearted. After Lambert's victory the local populace helped to round up the fugitives. The weak response in August 1659 has to be compared with the mounting popular enthusiasm for the king's cause in the following winter and spring, and the contrast is largely explained by the intervening events.

The defeat of Booth's rising removed the one serious check on the worsening relations between the army grandees and the Rump, which was even less inclined to admit them to any share of political authority than it had been in 1652–3. To explain the upheavals of the next few months would require a longer narrative than this brief survey can afford, but, to cut a long story short, the army interrupted the Rump again on 13 October, following a series of foolish provocations on both sides. After a fortnight in which they plainly did not know what to do next, the army officers set up a provisional government which called itself the Committee of Safety, but they could find no reputable politicians to join them. Worse still for them, General Monck threatened to bring the army that he commanded in Scotland to the support of the Rump. Lambert hastened north to assemble a force to oppose him, and a fresh civil war seemed a serious threat. England, especially London, began to slide down into anarchy. Citizens clashed violently with the troops, the central law courts ceased to sit, goldsmiths moved their stocks out of town, the apprentices demonstrated lustily and their elders threatened to pay no taxes until they were voted by a full and free parliament. Trade, which had slumped again after the relative prosperity of

Cromwell's Protectorate, ground towards a halt. By 26 December Fleetwood had had enough, and the now much shrunken Rump sneaked back to the Commons' House by back streets.

That was all that Monck had demanded, but he marched his army into England all the same, and reached London with it on 3 February. All along the way he received petitions for a full and free parliament, which were barely concealed calls for the restoration of the king. Whether he himself had made up his mind yet to declare for Charles II we cannot know, but if he had he was a stout liar. He probably kept more than one option open until the last moment. Haselrig thoroughly distrusted him, and the Rump promptly set Monck upon the unpopular task of punishing the city of London for its recent threats of resistance. After some hesitation, he did what many a pamphlet had been urging for weeks: he readmitted to parliament the 'secluded members' who had been debarred from sitting since Pride's Purge. At that point the Restoration became a certainty, for they easily outnumbered the surviving Rumpers, and since they had never wanted to depose Charles I they were all in favour of restoring Charles II. That evening the bells rang in every city steeple, and the bonfires in countless streets made the whole sky glow (7, 38).

The rest belongs to the story of the Restoration: the final self-dissolution of the Long Parliament on 16 March, the gathering tide of royalism in the elections to the Convention, the declaration of Breda and the proclamation of King Charles II on 8 May. Monarchism was triumphant, yet when the Protectorate had perished a year earlier it had fallen not to the royalists, but to its own radical opponents: the commonwealthsmen, the disaffected elements in the army and the sectarian extremists. The Rump, whose agents had exploited their discontents, had been quite unable (and largely unwilling) to satisfy their aspirations, and had proved even more politically bankrupt and nationally unpopular than in 1653. The fast rising flood of enthusiasm for the monarchy and the ancient constitution expressed a hankering for security and the rule of law. Both had suddenly become fragile, indeed had almost perished in the autumn and winter of 1659–60. The Restoration was necessary to fill a political vacuum, for the Commonwealth had collapsed inwards, destroyed by its own internal strife.

Bibliography

The following is a selection of recent and fairly recent works which bear particularly on points discussed in this pamphlet. The numbers are those by which they are referred to in the text.

Place of publication is London unless stated otherwise.

1 G. E. Aylmer, *The Levellers in the English Revolution* (1975).
2 G. E. Aylmer, *The State's Servants: the Civil Service of the English Republic 1649–1660* (1973).
3 G. E. Aylmer (ed.), *The Interregnum: the Quest for Settlement 1646–1660* (1972). The contributions referred to are by (a) J. P. Cooper, (b) Claire Cross, (c) Ivan Roots, (d) Keith Thomas, (e) David Underdown, (f) Austin Woolrych.
4 T. C. Barnard, *Cromwellian Ireland: English Government and Reform in Ireland, 1649–1660* (Oxford, 1975).
5 John Bossy, *The English Catholic Community 1570–1850* (1975).
6 B. S. Capp, *The Fifth Monarchy Men: a Study in Seventeenth-Century English Millenarianism* (1972).
7 Godfrey Davies, *The Restoration of Charles II 1658–1660* (Oxford, 1955).
8 F. D. Dow, *Cromwellian Scotland 1651–1660* (Edinburgh, 1979).
9 Alan Everitt, *The Community of Kent and the Great Rebellion 1640–1660* (Leicester, 1966).
10 Christopher Hill, *Antichrist in Seventeenth-Century England* (Oxford, 1971).
11 Christopher Hill, *God's Englishman: Oliver Cromwell and the English Revolution* (1970).
12 Christopher Hill, *The World Turned Upside Down: Radical Ideas During the English Revolution* (1972).

13 Derek Hirst, *The Representative of the People? Voters and Voting in England under the Early Stuarts* (Cambridge, 1975).

14 J. R. Jones, *Britain and the World 1649–1815* (1980).

15 Mark A. Kishlansky, *The Rise of the New Model Army* (Cambridge, 1979).

16 Mark A. Kishlansky, 'The case of the army truly stated: the creation of the New Model Army', *Past & Present* 81 (1978).

17 Mark A. Kishlansky, 'The army and the Levellers: the roads to Putney', *Historical Journal*, XXII (1979).

18 W. A. Lamont, *Godly Rule: Politics and Religion 1603–1660* (1969).

19 Olivier Lutaud, *Winstanley: Socialisme et Christianisme sous Cromwell* (Paris, 1976).

20 A. W. McIntosh, 'The numbers of the regicides', *History* LXVII (1982).

21 John Miller, *Popery and Politics in England 1660–1688* (Cambridge, 1973).

22 J. S. Morrill, *The Revolt of the Provinces: Conservatives and Radicals in the English Civil War, 1630–1650* (1976).

23 J. S. Morrill, 'Mutiny and discontent in English provincial armies, 1645–1647', *Past & Present* 56 (1972).

24 Michael Roberts, 'Cromwell and the Baltic', *English Historical Review* LXXVI (1961), reprinted in M. Roberts, *Essays in Swedish History* (1967).

25 Ivan Roots, *The Great Rebellion 1642–1660* (1966).

26 Ivan Roots, 'Swordsmen and decimators – Cromwell's Major-Generals', in R. H. Parry (ed.), *The English Civil War and After 1642–1658* (1970).

27 David Stevenson, *Revolution and Counter-Revolution in Scotland 1644–1651* (1977).

28 Murray Tolmie, *The Triumph of the Saints: the Separate Churches of London 1616–1649* (Cambridge, 1977).

29 David Underdown, *Pride's Purge: Politics in the Puritan Revolution* (Oxford, 1971).

30 David Underdown, *Royalist Conspiracy in England 1649–1660* (New Haven, Conn., 1960).

31 David Underdown, *Somerset in the Civil War and Interregnum* (1973).

32 David Underdown, '"Honest" radicals in the counties, 1642–1649', in D. Pennington and K. Thomas (eds), *Puritans and Revolutionaries: Essays in Seventeenth-Century History Presented to Christopher Hill* (Oxford, 1978).

33 Donald Veall, *The Popular Movement for Law Reform 1640–1660* (Oxford, 1970).

34 Charles Wilson, *Profit and Power: a Study of England and the Dutch Wars* (1957).

35 Gerrard Winstanley, *The Law of Freedom and Other Writings*, ed. Christopher Hill (1973).

36 Austin Woolrych, *Battles of the English Civil War* (1961).

37 Austin Woolrych, *Commonwealth to Protectorate* (Oxford, 1982).

38 Austin Woolrych, Introduction to *Complete Prose Works of John Milton*, VII (New Haven, Conn., revised ed. 1980).

39 Austin Woolrych, 'The calling of Barebone's Parliament', *English Historical Review* LXXX (1965).

40 Austin Woolrych, 'Milton and Cromwell', in M. Lieb and J. T. Shawcross (eds), *Achievements of the Left Hand: Essays on the Prose of John Milton* (Amherst, Mass., 1974).

41 Austin Woolrych, 'The Good Old Cause and the fall of the Protectorate', *Cambridge Historical Journal* XIII (1957).

42 Blair Worden, *The Rump Parliament 1648–1653* (Cambridge, 1974).

43 Blair Worden, 'The Bill for a New Representative: the dissolution of the Long Parliament, April 1653', *English Historical Review* LXXXVI (1971).